S

by Iain Gray

Lang**Syne**

PUBLISHING

WRITING *to* REMEMBER

Lang**Syne**

PUBLISHING

WRITING *to* REMEMBER

Strathclyde Business Centre
120 Carstairs Street, Glasgow G40 4JD
Tel: 0141 554 9944 Fax: 0141 554 9955
E-mail: info@scottish-memories.co.uk
www.langsyneshop.co.uk

Design by Dorothy Meikle
Printed by Thomson Litho, East Kilbride
© Lang Syne Publishers Ltd 2008

ISBN 1-85217-305-X

Sheridan

MOTTO:
The stag at bay becomes a lion.

CREST:
The head of a stag.

NAME variations include:
Ó Sirideáin (Gaelic),
O'Sheridan,
Sheridin,
Sheridon.

Chapter one:
Origins of Irish surnames

According to an old saying, there are two types of Irish – those who actually are Irish and those who wish they were.

This sentiment is only one example of the allure that the high romance and drama of the proud nation's history holds for thousands of people scattered across the world today.

It's a sad fact, however, that the vast majority of Irish surnames are found far beyond Irish shores, rather than on the Emerald Isle itself.

The population stood at around eight million souls in 1841, but today it stands at fewer than six million.

This is mainly a tragic consequence of the potato famine, also known as the Great Hunger, which devastated Ireland between 1845 and 1849.

The Irish peasantry had become almost wholly reliant for basic sustenance on the potato, first introduced from the Americas in the seventeenth century.

When the crop was hit by a blight, at least 800,000 people starved to death while an estimated two million others were forced to seek a new life far from their native shores – particularly in America, Canada, and Australia.

The effects of the potato blight continued until about 1851, by which time a firm pattern of emigration had become established.

Ireland's loss, however, was to the gain of the countries in which the immigrants settled, contributing enormously, as their descendants do today, to the well being of the nations in which their forefathers settled.

But those who were forced through dire circumstance to establish a new life in foreign parts never forgot their roots, or the proud heritage and traditions of the land that gave them birth.

Nor do their descendants.

It is a heritage that is inextricably bound up in the colourful variety of Irish names themselves – and the origin and history of these names forms an integral part of the vibrant drama that is the nation's history, one of both glorious fortune and tragic misfortune.

This history is well documented, and one of the most important and fascinating of the earliest sources are *The Annals of the Four Masters*, compiled between 1632 and 1636 by four friars at the Franciscan Monastery in County Donegal.

Compiled from earlier sources, and purporting to go back to the Biblical Deluge, much of the material takes in the mythological origins and history of Ireland and the Irish.

This includes tales of successive waves of invaders and settlers such as the Fomorians, the Partholonians, the Nemedians, the Fir Bolgs, the Tuatha De Danann, and the Laigain.

Of particular interest are the *Milesian Genealogies*,

because the majority of Irish clans today claim a descent from either Heremon, Ir, or Heber – three of the sons of Milesius, a king of what is now modern day Spain.

These sons invaded Ireland in the second millennium B.C, apparently in fulfilment of a mysterious prophecy received by their father.

This Milesian lineage is said to have ruled Ireland for nearly 3,000 years, until the island came under the sway of England's King Henry II in 1171 following what is known as the Cambro-Norman invasion.

This is an important date not only in Irish history in general, but for the effect the invasion subsequently had for Irish surnames.

'Cambro' comes from the Welsh, and 'Cambro-Norman' describes those Welsh knights of Norman origin who invaded Ireland.

But they were invaders who stayed, inter-marrying with the native Irish population and founding their own proud dynasties that bore Cambro-Norman names such as Archer, Barbour, Brannagh, Fitzgerald, Fitzgibbon, Fleming, Joyce, Plunkett, and Walsh – to name only a few.

These 'Cambro-Norman' surnames that still flourish throughout the world today form one of the three main categories in which Irish names can be placed – those of Gaelic-Irish, Cambro-Norman, and Anglo-Irish.

Previous to the Cambro-Norman invasion of the twelfth century, and throughout the earlier invasions and settlement of those wild bands of sea rovers known as the Vikings in the eighth and ninth centuries, the population of the island was relatively small, and it was normal for a person to be identified through the use of only a forename.

But as population gradually increased and there were many more people with the same forename, surnames were adopted to distinguish one person, or one community, from another.

Individuals identified themselves with their own particular tribe, or 'tuath', and this tribe – that also became known as a clann, or clan – took its name from some distinguished ancestor who had founded the clan.

The Gaelic-Irish form of the name Kelly, for example, is Ó Ceallaigh, or O'Kelly, indicating descent from an original 'Ceallaigh', with the 'O' denoting 'grandson of.' The name was later anglicised to Kelly.

The prefix 'Mac' or 'Mc', meanwhile, as with the clans of the Scottish Highlands, denotes 'son of.'

Although the Irish clans had much in common with their Scottish counterparts, one important difference lies in what are known as 'septs', or branches, of the clan.

Septs of Scottish clans were groups who often bore an entirely different name from the clan name but were under the clan's protection.

In Ireland, septs were groups that shared the same name and who could be found scattered throughout the four provinces of Ulster, Leinster, Munster, and Connacht.

The 'golden age' of the Gaelic-Irish clans, infused as their veins were with the blood of Celts, pre-dates the Viking invasions of the eighth and ninth centuries and the Norman invasion of the twelfth century, and the sacred heart of the country was the Hill of Tara, near the River Boyne, in County Meath.

Known in Gaelic as 'Teamhar na Rí', or Hill of Kings, it was the royal seat of the 'Ard Rí Éireann', or High King of Ireland, to whom the petty kings, or chieftains, from the island's provinces were ultimately subordinate.

It was on the Hill of Tara, beside a stone pillar known as the Irish 'Lia Fáil', or Stone of Destiny, that the High Kings were inaugurated and, according to legend, this stone would emit a piercing screech that could be heard all over Ireland when touched by the hand of the rightful king.

The Hill of Tara is today one of the island's main tourist attractions.

Opposition to English rule over Ireland, established in the wake of the Cambro-Norman invasion, broke out frequently and the harsh solution adopted by the powerful forces of the Crown was to forcibly evict the native Irish from their lands.

These lands were then granted to Protestant colonists, or 'planters', from Britain.

Many of these colonists, ironically, came from Scotland and were the descendants of the original 'Scotti', or 'Scots', who gave their name to Scotland after migrating there in the fifth century A.D., from the north of Ireland.

Colonisation entailed harsh penal laws being imposed on the majority of the native Irish population, stripping them practically of all of their rights.

The Crown's main bastion in Ireland was Dublin and its environs, known as the Pale, and it was the dispossessed peasantry who lived outside this Pale, desperately striving to eke out a meagre living.

It was this that gave rise to the modern-day expression of someone or something being 'beyond the pale'.

Attempts were made to stamp out all aspects of the ancient Gaelic-Irish culture, to the extent that even to bear a Gaelic-Irish name was to invite discrimination.

This is why many Gaelic-Irish names were anglicised with, for example, and noted above, Ó Ceallaigh, or O'Kelly, being anglicised to Kelly.

Succeeding centuries have seen strong revivals of Gaelic-Irish consciousness, however, and this has led to many families reverting back to the original form of their name, while the language itself is frequently found on the fluent tongues of an estimated 90,000 to 145,000 of the island's population.

Ireland's turbulent history of religious and political strife is one that lasted well into the twentieth century, a landmark century that saw the partition of the island into the twenty-six counties of the independent Republic of

Ireland, or Eire, and the six counties of Northern Ireland, or Ulster.

Dublin, originally founded by Vikings, is now a vibrant and truly cosmopolitan city while the proud city of Belfast is one of the jewels in the crown of Ulster.

It was Saint Patrick who first brought the light of Christianity to Ireland in the fifth century A.D.

Interpretations of this Christian message have varied over the centuries, often leading to bitter sectarian conflict – but the many intricately sculpted Celtic Crosses found all over the island are symbolic of a unity that crosses the sectarian divide.

It is an image that fuses the 'old gods' of the Celts with Christianity.

All the signs from the early years of this new millennium indicate that sectarian strife may soon become a thing of the past – with the Irish and their many kinsfolk across the world, be they Protestant or Catholic, finding common purpose in the rich tapestry of their shared heritage.

Chapter two:

In the face of invasion

The origins of the Sheridans in Ireland are lost in the swirling mists of Celtic time, but parting the complex genealogical veils it is possible to discern that they were first to be found in the area of Granard, in County Longford, in the northwest of the ancient province of Leinster.

It was in this territory – also known as Teffia, or Annaly, that the Ó Sirideáin flourished for a time in the distinguished role of erenaghs.

These were lay people who held the distinction of playing a special role in the religious life of the island – a position of trust that involved responsibility for helping to administer and oversee church land and property, while also affording them special privileges such as exemption from military service and church taxes.

But circumstances were destined to change dramatically for the clan, in common with other native Irish clans, in the destructive wake of the late twelfth century Cambro-Norman invasion of the island.

It was an invasion whose consequences for the future course of Ireland's history cannot be overestimated.

Twelfth century Ireland was far from being a unified nation, split up as it was into territories presided over by squabbling chieftains who ruled as kings in their own right – and this inter-clan rivalry worked to the advantage of the invaders.

In a series of bloody conflicts one chieftain, or king, would occasionally gain the upper hand over his rivals, and by 1156 the most influential was Muirchertach MacLochlainn, king of the powerful O'Neills of the province of Ulster.

He was opposed by the equally powerful Rory O'Connor, king of the province of Connacht, but he increased his power and influence by allying himself with Dermot MacMurrough, king of Leinster.

MacLochlainn and MacMurrough were aware that the main key to the kingdom of Ireland was the thriving trading port of Dublin that had been established by invading Vikings, or Ostmen, in 852A.D.

Their combined forces took Dublin, but when MacLochlainn died the Dubliners rose up in revolt and overthrew the unpopular MacMurrough.

A triumphant Rory O'Connor entered Dublin and was later inaugurated as Ard Rí, but MacMurrough refused to accept defeat.

He appealed for help from England's Henry II in unseating O'Connor, and the monarch agreed – but distanced himself from direct action by delegating his Norman subjects in Wales with the task.

These ambitious and battle-hardened barons and knights

had first settled in Wales following the Norman Conquest of England in 1066 and, with an eye on rich booty, plunder, and lands, were only too eager to obey their sovereign's wishes and furnish MacMurrough with aid.

He crossed the Irish Sea to Bristol, where he rallied powerful barons such as Robert Fitzstephen and Maurice Fitzgerald to his cause, along with Gilbert de Clare, Earl of Pembroke.

The mighty Norman war machine soon moved into action, and so fierce and disciplined was their onslaught on the forces of Rory O'Connor and his allies that by 1170 they had re-captured Dublin, in the name of MacMurrough, and other strategically important territories.

It was now that a nervous Henry II began to take cold feet over the venture, realising that he may have created a rival in the form of a separate Norman kingdom in Ireland.

Accordingly, he landed on the island, near Waterford, at the head of a large army in October of 1171 with the aim of curbing the power of his barons.

But protracted war was averted when the barons submitted to the royal will, promising homage and allegiance in return for holding the territories they had conquered in the king's name.

Henry also received the submission and homage of many of the Irish chieftains, tired as they were with internecine warfare and also perhaps realising that as long as they were rivals and not united they were no match for the powerful forces the English Crown could muster.

English dominion over Ireland was ratified through the Treaty of Windsor of 1175, under the terms of which Rory O'Connor, for example, was allowed to rule territory unoccupied by the Normans in the role of a vassal of the king.

Two years earlier, Pope Alexander III had given Papal sanction to Henry's dominance over Ireland, on condition that he uphold the rights of the Holy Roman Catholic Church and that chieftains such as O'Connor adhere rigorously to the oaths of fealty they had sworn to the English king.

But the land was far from unified, blighted as it was with years of warfare and smarting under many grievances.

There were actually three separate Irelands: the territories of the privileged and powerful Norman barons and their retainers, the Ireland of the disaffected Gaelic-Irish such as the Sheridans who held lands unoccupied by the Normans, and the Pale – comprised of Dublin itself and a substantial area of its environs ruled over by an English elite.

Many Irish clans were forced to seek a reluctant accommodation with the Crown as further waves of land-grabbing Anglo-Norman adventurers descended on the island, while many others found themselves gradually forced from their ancient territories.

Although the date is not known with any degree of
precision, it is thought to have been in the decades following
the Treaty of Windsor that the Sheridans were pushed
northeastwards from Co. Longford into the area of present
day Co. Cavan, in the province of Connacht – their
distinguished role as erenaghs now lost to them.

It was here that they were destined to infuse their already
rich heritage with that of the powerful Clan O'Reilly, whose
motto is 'Fortitude and prudence' and whose crest features
an oak tree entwined with a serpent.

It was also now that they truly lived up to their motto of
'The stag at bay becomes a lion.'

The area controlled by the O'Reillys, centred on
Balleyjamesduff, was also known as Breifne O'Reilly, or
East Breifne, with the territory controlled by their
neighbours and great rivals the O'Rourkes known as
Breifne O'Rourke – now Co. Leitrim.

This territorial division had resulted from a fierce battle
fought in 1256 between the O'Reillys and the O'Rourkes at
Ballinamore, a battle in which the Sheridans fought at the
side of the Reillys.

But many of the clans found themselves forced to sink
their differences in the face of the common foe – the English
Crown.

Chapter three:

Rebels and Jacobites

One graphic illustration of the harsh treatment meted out to the native Irish clans can be found in a desperate plea sent to Pope John XII by Roderick O'Carroll of Ely, Donald O'Neill of Ulster, and a number of other chieftains in 1318.

They stated: 'As it very constantly happens, whenever an Englishman, by perfidy or craft, kills an Irishman, however noble, or however innocent, be he clergy or layman, there is no penalty or correction enforced against the person who may be guilty of such wicked murder.

'But rather the more eminent the person killed and the higher rank which he holds among his own people, so much more is the murderer honoured and rewarded by the English, and not merely by the people at large, but also by the religious and bishops of the English race.'

The discontent boiled over in 1641 in the form of a rebellion by the Catholic landowners such as the O'Reillys and their Sheridan kinsfolk against the Crown's policy of settling, or 'planting' loyal Protestants on Irish land.

This policy had started during the reign from 1491 to 1547 of Henry VIII, whose Reformation had effectively outlawed the established Roman Catholic faith throughout his dominions.

This settlement of loyal Protestants in Ireland continued throughout the subsequent reigns of Elizabeth I, James I (James VI of Scotland), and Charles I.

In the insurrection that exploded in 1641, at least 2,000 Protestant settlers were massacred while thousands more were stripped of their belongings and driven from their lands.

Among the leaders of the rebellion in Co. Cavan was the Sheridan's overlord, Myles O'Reilly, better known to posterity by the rather more frightening name of Myles the Slasher.

In one particularly vicious encounter at Belturbet he had 60 hapless English settlers thrown over a bridge to drown in the river below; in the sickening tit-for-tat retaliation of the times, this only served to provoke revenge from the English forces in the form of 27 Irish natives being summarily put to the sword and 14 others hanged from the nearest trees.

The bold Myles the Slasher himself, keen-edged sword still in hand, was killed in 1644 while attempting to defend a vital river crossing.

Terrible as the atrocities against the Protestant settlers had undoubtedly been, subsequent accounts became greatly exaggerated, serving to fuel a burning desire on the part of Protestants for revenge against the rebels.

Tragically for Ireland, this revenge became directed not only against the rebels in particular, but the native Irish in general.

The English Civil War intervened to prevent immediate

action against the rebels, but following the execution of Charles I in 1649 and the consolidation of the power of England's Oliver Cromwell, the time was ripe was revenge.

The Lord Protector, as he was named, descended on Ireland at the head of a 20,000-strong army that landed at Ringford, near Dublin, in August of 1649.

The consequences of this Cromwellian conquest still resonate throughout the island today.

Cromwell had three main aims: to quash all forms of rebellion, to 'remove' all Catholic landowners who had taken part in the rebellion, and to convert the native Irish to the Protestant faith.

An early warning of the terrors that were in store for the native Catholic Irish came when the northeastern town of Drogheda was stormed and taken in September and between 2,000 and 4,000 of its inhabitants killed, including priests who were summarily put to the sword.

The Lord Protector soon held Ireland in a grip of iron, allowing him to implement what amounted to a policy of ethnic cleansing.

His troopers were given free rein to hunt down and kill priests, while Catholic estates were confiscated and an edict issued that any native Irish found east of the River Shannon after May 1, 1654 faced either summary execution or transportation to the West Indies.

Following the devastations that came in the wake of the Cromwellian invasion, the final death knell of the ancient

Gaelic order of proud native Irish clans such as the Sheridans was sounded.

This was in the form of what is known in Ireland as Cogadh an Dá Rí, or The War of the Two Kings.

Also known as the Williamite War in Ireland or the Jacobite War in Ireland, it was sparked off in 1688 when the Stuart monarch James II (James VII of Scotland) was deposed and fled into exile in France.

The Protestant William of Orange and his wife Mary (ironically a daughter of James II) were invited to take up the thrones of Scotland, Ireland, and England – but James still had significant support in Ireland.

His supporters were known as Jacobites, and among them was Thomas Sheridan, born in 1647.

Following the arrival in England of William and Mary from Holland, Richard Talbot, 1st Earl of Tyrconnell and James's Lord Deputy in Ireland, assembled an army loyal to the Stuart cause.

The aim was to garrison and fortify the island in the name of James and quell any resistance.

Londonderry, or Derry, proved loyal to the cause of William of Orange, or William III as he had become, and managed to hold out against a siege that was not lifted until July 28, 1689.

James, with the support of troops and money supplied by Louis XIV of France, had landed at Kinsale in March of 1689 and joined forces with his Irish supporters.

A series of military encounters followed, culminating in James's defeat by an army commanded by William at the battle of the Boyne on July 12, 1689.

James fled again into French exile, never to return, while another significant Jacobite defeat occurred in July of 1691 at the battle of Aughrim – with about half their army killed on the field, wounded, or taken prisoner.

The Williamite forces besieged Limerick and the Jacobites were forced into surrender in September of 1691.

A peace treaty, known as the Treaty of Limerick followed, under which those Jacobites willing to swear an oath of loyalty to William were allowed to remain in their native land.

Those reluctant to do so were allowed to seek exile on foreign shores, including Thomas Sheridan, who died in 1712.

His son, Sir Thomas Sheridan, who was born in 1684, served as tutor-in-exile at the Jacobite court in Rome to the young Charles Edward Stuart – better known to posterity as Bonnie Prince Charlie.

The prince landed on the small Outer Hebridean island of Eriskay on July 22, 1745, in a bid to restore the Stuart monarchy, arriving on the Scottish mainland at Loch nan Uamh three days later.

Among the small party who had sailed with him from France was Sir Thomas Sheridan, who served on his staff as his secretary.

The Stuart Standard was raised on August 19, at Glenfinnan, on Loch Shiel, and a Jacobite victory achieved at the battle of Prestonpans in September.

The confident prince, accompanied by Sir Thomas Sheridan, set off on the long march south to London to claim what was believed to be the rightful Stuart inheritance of the throne – but the army reached only as far as Derby before the controversial decision was taken to withdraw back over the border.

Jacobite hopes were dashed forever at the battle of Culloden, fought on Drummossie Moor, near Inverness, on April 16, 1746.

In what was the last major battle fought on British soil, hundreds of clansmen died on the battlefield while hundreds of others died later from their wounds and the brutal treatment of their government captors.

Among those forced to flee from the battlefield along with their prince was Sir Thomas Sheridan, who died in exile only a few weeks later.

His nephew, Chevalier Michael Sheridan, who was born in 1715 and died in 1775, had also taken part in the abortive '45 Rebellion.

Sheridans, meanwhile, were among the many thousands of Irish who were forced to seek a new life overseas during the famine known as The Great Hunger, caused by a failure of the potato crop between 1845 and 1849.

But in many cases Ireland's loss of sons and daughters such as the Sheridans was to the gain of those equally proud nations in which they settled.

Chapter four:

On the world stage

Bearers of the name of Sheridan have gained international acclaim in a diverse array of pursuits, not least in the world of acting.

Born Clara Lou Sheridan in 1915 in Denton, Texas, **Ann Sheridan** was launched on the path to international stardom through chance when her sister, unknown to her at the time, submitted a photograph of her to Paramount Pictures as a contestant in a beauty contest.

The flame haired beauty won the prize of a small part in a Paramount film, but received a much bigger role when she was cast in the 1934 *Search for Beauty*.

Lured to Warner Brothers in 1936 and changing her name from Clara Lou to Ann, she rapidly became a top sex symbol and starred in the 1938 *Angels with Dirty Faces* opposite James Cagney and the 1939 *Dodge City* opposite Errol Flynn.

Known as the Oomph Girl, she became a popular pin-up girl of American GIs during the Second World War, acting and singing in musicals such as the 1943 *Thank Your Lucky Stars* and the 1944 *Shine On, Harvest Moon*.

The actress, who died in 1967, has a star on the Hollywood Walk of Fame.

Born Dinah Mec in 1920 in Hampstead, London, **Dinah**

Sheridan is the veteran English actress whose first main role was in the 1953 film *Genevieve*.

Other notable roles include the mother in the 1970 *The Railway Children* and as Angela in the 1980s British sitcom *Don't Wait Up*.

Earning a Tony nomination in 1987 for his performance in a revival of the playwright Arthur Miller's *All My Sons*, **James Sheridan** is the American actor who was born in 1951 in Pasadena, California, while **Gail Sheridan**, born in 1916 in Seattle, Washington, was known as 'Hollywood's Kindest Actress.'

The actress, who died in 1982, was best known for her role in the 1930s Westerns *Hills of Wyoming* and *Hopalong Cassidy Returns*.

Born in 1947 **Susan Sheridan** is the British actress best known for her voice actress work in the role of Trillian in the popular radio series *The Hitchhiker's Guide to the Galaxy*.

Nicollete Sheridan, born in England in 1936 and who moved with her family to America when aged 12, is the actress who has appeared in a range of films and television soaps.

She is best known for her roles as Paige Matheson in *Knots Landing* and as Edie Britt in the *Desperate Housewives* series, for which she received a Golden Globe Award nomination in 2005 for Best Supporting Actress.

Starting her career as a dancer in musicals and nightclubs **Liz Sheridan**, born in 1929 in New York's

Westchester County, is the American actress who, in her early days, had a short-lived affair with the late screen icon James Dean.

Known for her role as the 'mother' of Jerry Seinfeld in the *Seinfeld* television series, she also appeared in other television series such as *Kojak*, *The A-Team*, *Moonlighting*, and *Cagney and Lacey*.

Behind the camera lens **Jim Sheridan**, born in Dublin in 1949, is the renowned Irish film director whose credits include the acclaimed *My Left Foot*, from 1989, the 1993 *In the Name of the Father*, the 2003 *In America*, and the 2005 *Get Rich or Die Tryin'*.

Bearers of the name of Sheridan have particularly excelled in the world of literature, no less so than the dynasty of literary Irish Sheridans whose most famous son was the playwright **Richard Brinsley Sheridan**.

Not only a playwright but a statesman, he was born in Dublin in 1751 and saw his first play, *The Rivals*, staged in 1775 at London's Covent Garden theatre.

His career as a playwright nearly ended as quickly as it had started as the play flopped on its opening night but, after casting another leading actor, it proved a resounding success.

His reputation firmly established, he went on to write what would become more famous plays, including *The School for Scandal* and *The Critic*, still performed to this day.

Entering the British Parliament in 1780, where he became a noted orator, he held high government posts that included Receiver-General of the Duchy of Cornwall and Treasurer of the Navy.

Despite his success he died in poverty in 1816, but was honoured by being interred in the Poet's Corner of London's Westminster Abbey.

His mother **Francis Sheridan** (née Chamberlaine), born in Dublin in 1724 and who died in 1766, was both a playwright and a novelist.

Her most successful novel was *Memoirs of Miss Sidney Bidulph*, while many of her plays were performed in London's famed Drury Lane theatre.

Her husband, and father of Richard Brinsley Sheridan, was the Irish actor and educationalist **Thomas Sheridan**, born in 1719 and who died in 1788.

The godson of the Irish-born satirist Jonathan Swift, he published a dictionary of the English language while also founding a school to teach 'young gentlemen' the rules of grammar.

Regarded as the leading ghost story writer of the nineteenth century **Joseph Sheridan Le Fanu** was a great-nephew of Richard Brinsley Sheridan.

Born in Dublin in 1814, he abandoned a career in law for journalism, submitting the first of his ghost tales to the Dublin University magazine in 1838.

His spooky tales such as *The Wyvern Mystery* are still

popular today, while his *Uncle Silas* was adapted for film in 1947, and adapted yet again in 1987 as *The Dark Angel*, starring Peter O'Toole.

He died in 1873.

Also in the literary sphere **John Desmond Sheridan**, born in 1903 and who died in 1980, was the distinguished Irish writer and humourist whose witty pieces for years graced the pages of the Irish Independent newspaper.

From literature to music **Tony Sheridan** is the English singer, songwriter, and guitarist who was born in Norwich in 1940.

He has the distinction of having played on early recordings of the Beatles when they performed in Hamburg.

Born in 1964 in Concord, New Hampshire, **Cosy Sheridan** is the American folk singer and songwriter famed for his musical treatment of issues such as the environment, and who released his *Live at Cederhouse* album in 2006.

In the highly competitive world of sport **Martin Sheridan**, born in 1881 in Treenduff, Co. Mayo, and who moved to the United States when aged 16, was the Irish-American athlete who became the holder of no less than five Olympic gold medals.

The athlete, who died in 1918, took gold in the discus throw in 1904, 1906, and 1908. He also took gold in 1906 for the shot put and in 1908 for the Greek discus.

On the cricket pitch **Keith Sheridan**, born in 1971 in Glasgow, is the Scottish cricketer who has, at the time of writing, played more than 80 times for his country, while in baseball **John F. Sheridan**, born in 1862 in Decatur, Illinois, and who died in 1914, was the Major League umpire who was named to the Roll of Honor of the Baseball Hall of Fame in 1946.

Born in 1964 in Stretford, England, of Irish descent, **John Sheridan** is the former professional footballer who won 34 caps playing for the Republic of Ireland team.

On the field of battle **Major General Philip Sheridan**, born in 1831 in Albany, New York, to Irish immigrant parents from Co. Cavan, was a leading Union Army officer during the American Civil War of 1861 to 1865.

He is also recognised as having been instrumental after the war in the development and protection of what is now the Yellowstone National Park.

Sheridan died in 1888, and his name is honoured through Yellowstone National Park's Mount Sheridan, the American Army M551 tank, Sheridan County, Montana, and Sheridan County, Wyoming.

But his memory is somewhat tarnished because of the infamous remark he is alleged to have made during the Indian Wars, that 'the only good Indians I ever saw were dead.'

In the world of politics **Tommy Sheridan** is the Scottish socialist politician who was born in Glasgow in 1964 and who was elected to the Scottish Parliament in 1999 for the Scottish Socialist Party.

Jailed on occasion for his opposition to the presence of the nuclear submarine fleet at the Faslane Naval Base on Scotland's west coast and for his opposition to the poll tax, he resigned from the Scottish Socialist Party in 2006 and formed the new socialist party Solidarity.

Sheridans have also been prominent in the world of science – particularly **Thomas B. Sheridan**, born in 1931 in Cincinnati.

Professor of Mechanical Engineering and Applied Psychology Emeritus at the world-renowned Massachusetts Institute of Technology, he is recognised as one of the world's leading pioneers of robotics and remote control technology.

Key dates in Ireland's history from the first settlers to the formation of the Irish Republic:

circa 7000 B.C.	Arrival and settlement of Stone Age people.
circa 3000 B.C.	Arrival of settlers of New Stone Age period.
circa 600 B.C.	First arrival of the Celts.
200 A.D.	Establishment of Hill of Tara, Co. Meath, as seat of the High Kings.
circa 432 A.D.	Christian mission of St. Patrick.
800-920 A.D.	Invasion and subsequent settlement of Vikings.
1002 A.D.	Brian Boru recognised as High King.
1014	Brian Boru killed at battle of Clontarf.
1169-1170	Cambro-Norman invasion of the island.
1171	Henry II claims Ireland for the English Crown.
1366	Statutes of Kilkenny ban marriage between native Irish and English.
1529-1536	England's Henry VIII embarks on religious Reformation.
1536	Earl of Kildare rebels against the Crown.
1541	Henry VIII declared King of Ireland.
1558	Accession to English throne of Elizabeth I.
1565	Battle of Affane.
1569-1573	First Desmond Rebellion.
1579-1583	Second Desmond Rebellion.
1594-1603	Nine Years War.
1606	Plantation' of Scottish and English settlers.
1607	Flight of the Earls.
1632-1636	Annals of the Four Masters compiled.
1641	Rebellion over policy of plantation and other grievances.
1649	Beginning of Cromwellian conquest.
1688	Flight into exile in France of Catholic Stuart monarch James II as Protestant Prince William of Orange invited to take throne of England along with his wife, Mary.
1689	William and Mary enthroned as joint monarchs; siege of Derry.
1690	Jacobite forces of James defeated by William at battle of the Boyne (July) and Dublin taken.

1691	Athlone taken by William; Jacobite defeats follow at Aughrim, Galway, and Limerick; conflict ends with Treaty of Limerick (October) and Irish officers allowed to leave for France.
1695	Penal laws introduced to restrict rights of Catholics; banishment of Catholic clergy.
1704	Laws introduced constricting rights of Catholics in landholding and public office.
1728	Franchise removed from Catholics.
1791	Foundation of United Irishmen republican movement.
1796	French invasion force lands in Bantry Bay.
1798	Defeat of Rising in Wexford and death of United Irishmen leaders Wolfe Tone and Lord Edward Fitzgerald.
1800	Act of Union between England and Ireland.
1803	Dublin Rising under Robert Emmet.
1829	Catholics allowed to sit in Parliament.
1845-1849	The Great Hunger: thousands starve to death as potato crop fails and thousands more emigrate.
1856	Phoenix Society founded.
1858	Irish Republican Brotherhood established.
1873	Foundation of Home Rule League.
1893	Foundation of Gaelic League.
1904	Foundation of Irish Reform Association.
1913	Dublin strikes and lockout.
1916	Easter Rising in Dublin and proclamation of an Irish Republic.
1917	Irish Parliament formed after Sinn Fein election victory.
1919-1921	War between Irish Republican Army and British Army.
1922	Irish Free State founded, while six northern counties remain part of United Kingdom as Northern Ireland, or Ulster; civil war up until 1923 between rival republican groups.
1949	Foundation of Irish Republic after all remaining constitutional links with Britain are severed.